HOLDING ON

Belinda Rimmer

NEW WALK EDITIONS
Leicester & Nottingham

Acknowledgements

Some of these poems first appeared in the following print and online journals: *Nine Muses Poetry*, *Prole*, *Burnt Breakfast*, *Acumen* and *The Lake*. My thanks to the editors involved. 'Circa 1979' was long-listed in the National Poetry Competition in 2020. 'Being Swedish in Pontlottyn' was a joint runner-up in the Stanza Poetry Competition in 2019. Thank you also to my poetry workshopping group and to Nick Everett for his editorial input.

978-1-8381153-5-7

Belinda Rimmer has asserted her right under Section 77 of the Copyright, Designs and Patents Act 1988 to be identified as the sole author of this work.

Published by New Walk Editions
c/o Nick Everett, Centre for New Writing,
University of Leicester, LE1 7RH
and
c/o Rory Waterman
Nottingham Creative Writing Hub,
Nottingham Trent University, NG11 8NS

www.newwalkmagazine.com

Printed by imprintdigital, Upton Pyne, Exeter.

Contents

Circa 1979   *5*
Bank Nurse   *7*
Saturdays at the Piccadilly   *8*
The Wolves   *9*
Something Opening   *10*
Being Swedish in Pontlottyn   *11*
Liz Berry Reads 'Bird'   *12*
Grief and Forgiveness   *13*
A Child   *14*
Missing Flowers   *15*
Liaison   *16*
Holding On   *17*
On a Curving Beach   *18*
Question Marks   *19*
Are you Talking?   *20*
Turning Point   *21*

Circa 1979

He'd picked you
off the dance floor, except he hadn't
walked you home. It was an alley,

cleaner than some. You remember
a cluster of leaves, autumn,
and Kit Kat wrappers

flickering red/silver.
His arms encircled, or pinned
you to the wall. Rain dripped

on your shoes.
You didn't know
how to say *stop*, or if you did

you didn't say it,
or maybe you said it
but it didn't sound right.

Maybe you didn't want it
to stop in the clean alley
with the glinting Kit Kat wrappers.

You'd become separated
from your shoes. You might
have pushed him away,

but you don't think so.
It became noisy, your shoes
on the other side of the alley.

You might have been shouting,
shouting something. *Unreasonable*,
he might have said.

Maybe you were paying
attention to the rain,
thinking about *Grease*, the musical,

or how your dad always bought you
a Kit Kat on his way home from work.

Bank Nurse

I hand her a glowing cocktail
of anti-psychotic, sleeping and vitamin tablets.

Fuck off, she says. She likes her voices.
They tell her she looks pretty in yellow.

A slammed door. She's halfway down
the hospital corridor

on her way to the wood.
I've been told to let her go –

a gust of fresh air,
a dusting of sun, and she'll be back.

But I find myself among the trees
with the foraging blackbirds and bluebell shoots.

And there she is, hanging
from a branch like a bat,

dress over her head,
scratches on her bark-brown legs.

Sensing me,
she shimmies down the trunk.

Together we walk back through the wood
and I hear her voices speak of love.

Saturdays at the Piccadilly –

sudden and loud, sharp-edged,
of glass, of knives, and fingernails.

Boys, twitchy, tasting of aftershave,
broke chairs, each other; grew scars.

I haunted the dance floor,
Rock Your Baby,

always the last to leave,
to slip on a coat and go home

along Kingfisher Drive,
the sky spinning.

If my hair held the memory
of smoke, I'd wear a ponytail

to school, sit at the back of class.
This was 1970s' Swindon.

When someone daubed SLAG
on the chip shop wall,

I didn't yet know how a word
could take a body down.

The Wolves

i.m. Eleanor Farjeon, 1881-1965

As a child, I did not like to be prised open,
for the wolves inside me to be snared or cornered.

If I caught glimpses of my animals,
the way they carried their young

or passed through shadowy landscapes,
I was not disquieted;

they made no demands,
did not crush or hurt me.

Sometimes, in the middle of a turbulent night,
I would catch their scent,

the earthy richness of it,
and feel less alone.

Something Opening

after Eleanor Farjeon's account of her childhood in The Little Bookroom *(1955)*

I could not leave my hideaway
behind the house

until the whole garden had been read –
flowers became bearded ladies, thistles woven clouds.

Between the rocks magic peacock feathers appeared.
In this place fairies sang in their loudest voices.

If my father passed by on his way to tea,
or my brothers, in a game of pursuit,

came too close, I did not move,
not even to push up my glasses.

I was drab as a moth, invisible,
alone but not lonely,

waiting to court the grass with kisses,
to drink rain, to be

on the other side of everything.

Being Swedish in Pontlottyn

for Maria Evans

Word goes around: *Maria's friend is Swedish.*
Boys in stripy tops line up
across the dance floor curious
to know if my life is all sex and cigarettes.
They tie themselves in knots
to get close to me. I make space
between my lips to let out the nonsense
of pretend Swedish. I tell them of forests,
herds of moose, the way to smoke a herring.
The boys wrap me in their heat,
their beery breath, their rugby thighs.
They hang on to my every word.
Later, on the train home,
when I ask for *a single to Gloucester, please,*
there's a dead feeling on my tongue.

Liz Berry Reads 'Bird'

Her words strap me to the chair,
tight as bath-shrunk Levis.

She seems far away,
beyond this stifling room
at the back of an Oxfam bookshop.

Her arms stir, a bristle of her chest
into winter plumage,
a click, click, click of lips
sharpening to beak.

She lifts, perches on shelves
and hardback Harry Potters,
moulting little downy wisps,
transforming from hummingbird to lark to wren.

After the poem ends, she's still catching
delicate draughts. At the book signing,
I steal a feather from her wing.

Grief and Forgiveness

Barely a single memory of their camping trip,
just the appearance of a deer and her fawn,
and how there was nothing
to do but make love.

When he brought her a coffee
and she opened her bag and vomited
into the clutter of hairpins and dried up lipsticks
she knew at once,

and it wasn't funny
or pleasant, it was terrifying.
Before she'd even finished telling him he'd left.

It was summer, scorching
and bothersome with flies,
when the baby came.

Each day she brushed her hair
and went into town,
to be anywhere except where it mattered.

A Child

stands outside my kitchen window
in a sudden burst of rain
as dye from her dress –
bluer than cold skin or sky –
starts running down her legs
and collecting on the pavement.

She dabs herself with a tissue
to stem the flood, reaches down
to feather the blue into wings.

Her mother comes splashing
up the road all
where have you been?
and slaps and kisses.

For days after, I can't stop thinking
about the dress, its patches
of pure white purged of blue.

Missing Flowers

after Edward Hopper's Room in New York *(1932)*

Her husband doesn't ask
where his bouquet has gone.

She doesn't tell him –
thrown into a bin.

Tomorrow, from the garden,
she'll pick her own bunch, set it back on the table.

The music and tapping feet of tonight's theatre
have danced her to the piano.

She's hunched on a child's music stool,
her dress, red as theatre roses, as stage blood,

twisted and bunched,
her skin blubber-white in the street light.

She can't make anything sing
with her tangerine bulges for hands.

But her daughter's baby fingers
dance across the keys.

Should she wake her
and call her downstairs?

Should she wake her
with a plunk, plunk, plunk on the piano?

She should wake the whole house.

Liaison

We had agreed to meet by a river
beside three boulders.

I was to bring a picnic, and he a blanket.

I had gone along the road
signposted *Unsuitable for Motors*,
as instructed, followed a rough track
and stopped to watch a heron sulkily
paddling in an old mill pond.

I caught sight of him then
through summer's rusty haze.
He held a bunch of daisies.

I raced back to my car, fell into the familiar clutter
of children's books and empty crisp packets.

Sometimes I return to the river –
let ghosts drift by
with their wounds of daisies.

Holding On
after Jane Commane's poem, 'On the New Bypass'

In a quiet place
with the solemn oath of a stream,

a hedgerow the length of a field,
meadows wild and free

where skies fall into shape,
into blue,

is the last tree standing.
A shiver of pink blossom,

bark rough and ragged as a fisherman's hands.
A girl sits among its branches

like a bird,
excited by the smell of leaves and rain.

She's watching out
for changes in rhythm or weather,

clinging on
with the arms of a panicked child,

clinging on
to the last tree standing.

On a Curving Beach
in memory of Benjamin Sayers, 1933-1999

My father's in a white vest,
hair slicked back.
I'm in a knitted bikini,
digging in the sand.

I unearth a shell.
My father jokes it's radioactive,
bluer than the word
blue written in a blue pen.

He holds it to his ear to hear a cathedral choir.
I hear seabirds learning the language of waves.

All day we feast on its blueness,
make plans to hang it from the apple tree,
the one we planted from a pip.

But it ends up on a bathroom ledge
until it bleaches to a grubby grey.
No moment of loss, just a gradual fading,

as if this were never our shell
and we had never spoken

so highly of blue.

Question Marks
i.m. Melanie Klein, 1882-1960

Melanie, a gloved hand neatly in her lap,
tightly laced boots peeking from her dress
like question marks, is looking away
from the camera to something in the distance –
her dreams of medicine, of the mind.

Simple, to fall in love, to drop her ambitions
all in one go, to be awoken in love.
But now they rarely touch,
the slightest opinion he shoots her down.

*

One corner of the room to another,
she's arranging her little wooden figures, her bricks,
her sticks of chalk, pots of paint, paper and clay.
When the children come they bring minds
like vast skies of guilt and joy and grief,
of fear and love and envy.

*

She barely felt the knife,
but it must have touched her
there and there.

She tries to take an interest
in the people arriving with flowers
but is cold, too much in pain.

She swirls her loose hair
into a French plait, pins and pins.
Then the nurse brings a bowl of soapy water

to wash with gentle hands
between the buckles of her skin.

Are You Talking?

Railway scratches on her arms,
she traces the thickest to its terminus.
Gloucester, she jokes.

I search in my bag for Savlon.
White cream settles
like snail-tracks in sunlight.

The sessions transport her
from school to a room with a ticking clock
and a window onto the hill.

Her hill. She could map it,
she says, all the landmarks.

I give her paper, pencil, crayons.
She draws trees, a stream, a washpool,
grazing fields, none of it to scale,

but not the spot where her father beat her,
stains now washed away. Near the quarry,

she crayons an abandoned van – patches of rust,
faint yellow paint, smashed glass –
and birds perched in lines.

I can imagine it, I say, under a half-moon.
She tells me, but a full moon is better.

Turning Point

My son and I are remembering his birthday party
when a girl ran into our patio window
bashing her head enough to bleed.

We're not laughing at the girl
but at the hats I'd made from old comics
none of the children would wear.

And then the girl running into the window
reminds us of the homing pigeons
that flew over our house every day.

We'd stand to count them,
arms outstretched, and listen
for the swimming-under-water sound of their wings.

I was fascinated by their pull toward home,
my son with the things you could make from birds' bones
and the place where the pigeons turned.